MW01065270

Why I Love My
MOM

101 Dang Good Reasons

Ellen Patrick

ISBN: 1-58173-403-4

Jacket and text design by Miles G. Parsons
Printed in Italy

1. Where else would I get something good to eat, any time of day or night?

2. You understand me.

—ᨑᨑᨑ—

3. Even at my worst, you're there for me.

4. Can you say "unconditional love"?

5. I don't like to admit it, but you really do know best.

6. World's best shoulder to cry on.

7. World's best hug.

—⁓—

8. World's best kiss to make it better.

9. World's best juggler.

—◆◆◆—

10. World's best diplomat.

11. World's best cook.

12. World's best teacher.

—⁓—

13. World's greatest general.

14. You taught me how to say please and thank you.

15. You taught me how to stand up straight.

—◊—

16. You taught me to be proud of who I am.

17. Can you say forgiveness?

—⁘—

18. You can always make me laugh.

19. Can you say trust?

—m—

20. It wouldn't be home without you.

21. I can tell you anything (well, almost).

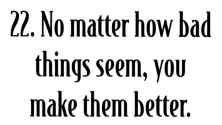

22. No matter how bad
things seem, you
make them better.

—∽—

23. You know when
NOT to laugh.

24. You know how to make my tears go away.

—⚭—

25. Even my friends all love you.

26. If there were an Academy Award for patience, you'd win it.

27. You should win the Nobel Peace Prize.

—∿∿—

28. As long as I have you, there's nothing I can't do.

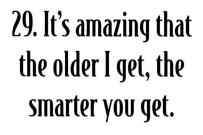

29. It's amazing that the older I get, the smarter you get.

30. I don't know why you picked me to be your kid, but I'm glad you did.

31. You never forget my birthday.

—∞—

32. You make me take my medicine.

33. You always know when I need a special treat.

34. You're always on my side.

—∿—

35. I know you'll wait up for me.

36. When you say it's for my own good, you're usually right.

37. You're psychic.

—✺—

38. You're pretty.

—✺—

39. You're generous.

40. You're kind.

41. You're always one step ahead of me.

42. You're funny.

—⫘—

43. You're sweet.

—⫘—

44. You're you.

45. Out of all the moms in the world, I'm glad I picked you.

46. Who else would do my laundry for me?

47. Who else would help me with my homework?

—⚯—

48. Who else would yell at me, then kiss and hug me?

49. Who else would tell me to get a haircut (and I would listen)?

50. Who else would give me a ride when I desperately need one?

51. Who else would give me a little help in the financial department?

52. Who else would comfort me when I have a nightmare?

—∞—

53. Who else would look under my bed for the bogeyman?

54. Who else would take care of me when I'm sick?

55. Who else would stick up for me (even when I'm wrong)?

—⁓—

56. Who else would worry about me?

57. I can't imagine a world without you, Mom.

58. I feel sorry for all those other kids who don't have you as their mom.

59. You should be president.

—ɷ—

60. You should be the queen of the world.

61. You should at least be mayor.

62. You should wear a crown and eat cake every day.

63. I love you more than the sky is blue.

—⧓—

64. I love you even when I don't like you!

65. You sure know how to break up a fight.

66. You sure know how to put on a Band-Aid.

67. You sure know
how to tell people
what is what.

68. You make me eat right.

———ɷ———

69. You make me work hard.

70. You taught me the difference between right and wrong.

71. You taught me how to treat people.

72. You taught me to dream.

—⧓—

73. You let me have fun.

74. You gave me all my favorite memories.

—⁓—

75. You give me everything important in life.

76. You help keep me out of trouble.

―◆―

77. You taught me to tell the truth.

78. You have the world's biggest heart.

79. You make the world's best dinner.

—∿∿—

80. You take me out for burgers and fries.

81. I don't think there is anything you can't do.

82. You seem to get more done every day than other people.

83. It seems like you are always right – eventually.

84. There is nothing better than coming home to my mom.

—◆◆◆—

85. Sometimes I think you are the only person I can talk to.

86. You buy me things even when you can't afford it.

87. You always like my presents.

88. You never laugh at me, just with me.

—⁓—

89. I think you are pretty cool, even if I never tell you.

90. You are my best friend.

91. You are my role model.

—⁓—

92. You are my favorite older person (even though you are NOT old)!

93. You are my life preserver.

94. You are my back-up plan.

—∿—

95. You are my rock.

96. You are my inspiration.

97. You gave me my heart and soul.

98. You gave me my walking-around sense.

—⁂—

99. You gave me this wonderful thing called life.

100. I can never thank you enough for everything you do for me.

101. All I can say is, you are my favorite mom in the whole entire world.